# The King is Coming

*Pray for the Peace of Jerusalem:*
*A Divine Way for a Blessed Life*

## Sam Dewald Stephen

# Dedication

I dedicate this book to those who have
laid down their lives over the past
to pray and work for the peace of Jerusalem,
to bring glory to our God of Israel,
our Jewish Messiah Jesus Christ
and God the Holy Spirit.

# Table of Contents

# Endorsements

Pastor Sam Dewald is uniquely qualified to usher us into *the blessings of the Lord.* In this new book *The King is Coming-Pray for the Peace of Jerusalem,* Pastor Sam carefully leads his readers through the pages of scripture, history and current events. Like a master artist, he paints a vivid, detailed picture for anyone to easily see and captures the heart of God for His people, His land and Jerusalem. Within these pages, I found an important revelation of *God's blessing* upon those who love His people, His nation and speak peace over Jerusalem. I encourage the personal activation of this message, as we join in praying for the peace of Jerusalem.

Apostle Elaine C. Rumley,
President
Eagles World Intercessors Inc

This valuable book reveals the Biblical importance and uniqueness of Israel. Pastor Sam Dewald does an excellent job in communicating why we should pray for the City of Jerusalem. Supporting Israel opens the channels of God's blessings not only for you, but also for your city and your nation. When you pray for Israel, you are actually preparing the way for and ushering in the coming of the King.

Every Christian should have this book in their library, as well as in their hearts.

Lisa Depew
Texas State Coordinator
The Day of Prayer for the Peace of Jerusalem

# Foreword

As a former student at Christ for the Nations Institute ('83 grad) I discovered that I could not help but receive the impact of Gordon and Freda Lindsay's hearts regarding Israel. We studied Israel in prophesy and learned what God's Word said about it. We sat under Shira Soko Ram (Carole Lindsay), Gordon and Freda's daughter's teaching as well. CFNI has undertaken a large amount of outreach over the years to minister and pray for the peace of Jerusalem. Pastor Sam Dewald is one of those with a Pioneer's Spirit. He has not only prayed and ministered in Israel for years now, but he is also leading healing and prayer teams from the United States to join with other brothers and sisters in the congregations to bring the Kingdom of God and

His miraculous gifts of the spirit for "such a time as this"! He is a wonderful connector, bringing many from around the world who love Israel and pray.

Rev. Alta Hatcher
Director of Healing Ministries
Christ for the Nations

# Introduction

As we all await the coming of our Lord Jesus Christ, it is imperative to know the importance of praying for the peace of Jerusalem. It is the command of our Lord to every Bible believing Jew and Gentile. Many of us know that we should pray for the peace of Jerusalem, since we have read Psalm 122:6-7. Praise God for the many Christians around the world who are faithfully praying. But, there are still millions who do not have this revelation of the importance of praying for the peace of Jerusalem.

While I was living in Jerusalem and involved in a twenty-four hour prayer and intercession ministry, God began to show me the importance of praying for the peace of Jerusalem. As I was living in Jerusalem, many people asked me, "Why should I pray for the peace of Jerusalem?" This has led me into a deeper quest to dig into the Bible, pray, and seek Him for the real, divine reason.

God began to reveal from Scripture the reason why Christians should pray for the peace of Jerusalem and how it affects our lives and the entire world. I began to understand that praying for the peace of Jerusalem is directly connected to the coming of our Lord Jesus Christ. I was thrilled and fully persuaded to stand in support of Israel and to pray for the peace of Jerusalem with commitment. Since then, God has been using me to bring this revelation to the body of Christ.

As you prayerfully read through this book, I firmly believe that God will stir you up to:
- hunger for Him,
- desire to pray for the peace of Jerusalem, and
- stand in support of Israel like never before.

Be assured, as you pray for the peace of Jerusalem, you are close to the heart of God. Also, you will experience spiritual and personal breakthroughs. The true way to prosperity is to obey God and do what He has commanded us to do.

*"Pray for the peace of Jerusalem: 'May they prosper who love you. Peace be within your walls, Prosperity within your palaces.'"*
*(Psalm 122:6-7)*

As for my house and me, we see no other choice to serve the Lord and to pray for Jerusalem, Jews, and Israel to usher in Lord Jesus Christ's coming. I want to be close to the heart of God more than anything. Therefore, I choose with honor, to stand in the gap for Israel, Jews and Jerusalem with the love of Christ.

Shalom and Blessings!
Sam Dewald Stephen

## Chapter One

# Biblical Importance and Uniqueness of Israel

As we begin to learn the importance of praying for the peace of Jerusalem, it is vital to know the Biblical importance and uniqueness of the land of Israel, the Jewish people, and the city of Jerusalem. When we read the Bible in light of this revelation, it illuminates the Scripture and impacts our spiritual life and our walk with the Lord. Everything began and will end in the land of Israel. The culmination of our faith and of this age will come to an end there, ushering in the glorious millennial rule of Jesus Christ and then eternity.

## Uniqueness of Israel

Israel is the name of the nation covenanted and title deeded by the Creator of heaven and earth to the descendants of Abraham, Isaac, and Jacob. Israel is called the Holy Land in the Bible. Understanding Israel will help us to have a clear

> He brought them to the border of his holy land, to this land of hills he had won for them.
> Psalm 78:55 (NLT)

understanding of the Bible. Our God is called *The Holy One of Israel* or *The Lord God of Israel* in many Scriptures in the Bible.

David, while he was praying to God, spoke these words:

"And who is like Your people Israel, the one nation on the earth whom God went to redeem for Himself as a people – to make for Yourself a name by great and awesome deeds, by driving out nations from before Your people whom You redeemed from Egypt."

(1 Chronicles 17:21)

This strategically places l
position in the Bible, in Go
mately, in the world, espec
times. Israel is the piece of
that God has chosen for Hi

"For the LORD has chosen Zion; He has
desired it for His dwelling place: This is My
resting place forever; Here I will dwell, for I
have desired it." (Psalm 132:13- 14)

The Creator of heaven and earth chose Zion the
Holy Mountain, in the city of Jerusalem in the land
of Israel. He will dwell there forever. The coming
of our Lord Jesus is very, very near. It is best to get
acquainted with the land where He is going to dwell
and rule the earth for 1000 years.

I am excited to even hear the name Israel, as it
is our Lord's nation. I hope you feel the same way
too and experience this excitement. Join me as we
dig deeper about the importance of Israel. The word
'Israel' is mentioned approximately 2303 times in
the New King James Version of the Bible. I pray that
the Bible believing Jews and Christians will learn

ance of this nation. If the Holy Spirit has
ned it so many times in the Scriptures, it is
that we give due attention to it.

## The Most Central Point on the Earth

Israel is mentioned as the center of the earth in
the Scripture. Interestingly, Israel has also become
the center of attention in these end times as a prophetic fulfillment.

"...to seize spoil and carry off plunder, to
turn your hand against the waste places that
are now inhabited, and the people who were
gathered from the nations, who have acquired
livestock and goods, who dwell at the center
of the earth" (Ezekiel 38:12 ESV)

While I was living in Israel, whenever we planned
to travel to far off nations, it seemed to be equidis-
tant from Israel. For example, the flying hours from
Israel to Australia towards the east and the flying
hours from Israel to USA towards the west seemed
to be the same. It makes sense, right? Geographical

experts may disagree; and, I leave it to their own discretion. However, the oldest book in the Bible, the book of Job, described the earth as being round before any scientist figured it out.

In ancient times, maps displayed Jerusalem as the center of the earth. Our God has rightly chosen the center of the earth to be His headquarters to rule the earth during the millennium. The gospel went forth from the center of earth to the nations. I believe the gospel is coming back from the ends of the nations to the land of Israel, culminating in a powerful end time revival in Israel, ushering in the rapture and eventually, the millennium.

**The Glory of All Lands**

The Bible describes Israel as the glory of all lands. The Lord's glory was manifest in such a powerful way in Solomon's Temple. God chose this land to reveal His glory to the nations.

"So I also raised My hand in an oath to them in the wilderness, that I would not bring them into the land which I had given them, 'flowing with milk and honey,' <u>the glory of all lands.</u>"

(Ezekiel 20:15)

During the millennium, Israel will be the permanent place of God's glory, as the King of Glory – Jesus Christ will be ruling the whole earth from there. His glory will radiate from Israel and we,

> "And have made us kings and priests to our God; And we shall reign on the earth." Revelation 5:10

with our glorious bodies, will reign as kings and priests with Christ Jesus.

"Blessed and holy is he who has part in the first resurrection. Over such the second death has no power, but they shall be priests of God and of Christ, and shall reign with Him a thousand years." (Revelation 20:6)

## The Land Where the Bible Stories Took Place

- The majority of the Bible stories took place in Israel.
- The great miracles of Elijah and Elisha took place here.
- The great prophets like Samuel, Isaiah, Jeremiah,

and Ezekiel lived here.

- Powerful prophecies were spoken from this nation.
- Great and supernatural wars were battled in this nation.
- The ultimate war before the second coming of our Lord will be fought in Israel.
- The great King David wrote the amazing Psalm from this nation.
- The Psalm still resonates powerfully as a great tool to praise the Lord, as a powerful proclamation and as a great comfort for the people in sorrow.

## Jesus Christ, the Greatest Citizen of Israel

When God, who created heaven and earth, came to this earth to redeem the mankind, He chose Israel as the nation to be born in. He was the great Jewish Rabbi, the greatest citizen of Israel, who ever lived. What a glorious privilege for the nation of Israel to experience the soles of the feet of the Son of God to touch its ground.

Jesus was born, lived, ministered, crucified and

resurrected from this nation. He will also come back and rule the whole earth from this nation. Hallelujah!

## Israel a Nation with a Prophetic Destiny

The only nation on earth whose entire history is prophesied is the nation of Israel. God's faithfulness to this nation is what keeps it under Jewish rule, despite many wars and conflicts to gain control over this nation. God gave this land to the descendants of Abraham, Isaac, and Jacob. When the Israelites settled in this land, after the exodus from Egypt, Jewish monarchy was established through Saul.

Israel thrived during the rule of King David and Solomon as one undivided kingdom, Judah and Israel. Due to their disobedience, as predicted by the prophets, the nation was conquered and ruled by many, including:

- Babylonians,
- Assyrians,
- Persians,
- Hasmoneans,
- Romans,

- Byzantines,
- Arabs,
- Crusaders,
- Malmuk,
- Ottoman, and finally
- the British.

The Israelites were scattered all over the world. It is amazing even to think of how a tiny nation could survive all of these conquests; and yet, it is now the only thriving democracy in the Middle East. It is

> A nation re-established in one day.

just the act of a faithful God, the Holy one of Israel. On May 14, 1948, Israel was re-established as a nation by the miracle power of God, in one day. This was also prophesied in Isaiah 66:8:

"Who has heard such a thing? Who has seen such things? Shall the earth be made to give birth in one day? [Or] shall a nation be born at once? For as soon as Zion was in labor, She gave birth to her children."

Since the re-establishment, God has been so faithful in keeping this nation intact. Almost every day, many terrorist organizations around the world are trying to destroy this nation and completely wipe it off of the map of the world. According to Scripture, it will yet, once again go through much tribulation during what is called 'The time of Jacob's trouble,' as predicted in Jeremiah 30:4-7, Daniel 12:1, and Matthew 24:15-22. Then, Jesus himself will come as King of kings, destroy its enemies, and establish the Messianic rule from Jerusalem.

What a mighty God we serve! It is by His Word that everything is established, sustained and will end, ushering in a glorious millennium and eternity.

## The Nation Where Every Tribe and Tongue Will Gather

Israel is the nation where every tribe and tongue will go during the millennium to worship the King Jesus. Every nation will go to Israel to worship Jesus and keep the Feast of Tabernacles.

"And it shall come to p'
is left of all the nations ·
Jerusalem shall go up from
worship the King, the LORD o·
keep the Feast of Tabernacles."

Zecharia.

What a joy to behold the beauty of the .
in Israel and celebrate the Feast of Tabernacle.
during the 1000 year rule of our Lord Jesus Christ! I
encourage you to pray and get acquainted, even now,
with a tour that takes people to celebrate the most
joyful Jewish feast, the Feast of Tabernacles. God
instituted this feast to teach us about the millennial
rule of Jesus Christ. This feast will be fulfilled, when
Jesus comes back and rules from Israel.

I hope this teaching enlightened you and revealed
the importance and uniqueness of Israel. I pray that
God will give you a hunger to learn more about
Israel and to stand in support of this nation at these
crucial end times. If you want to be close to the heart
of God, listen to His heart cry and take a stand to be
a watchman/woman for Israel!

# Chapter Two

# The Biblical Importance and Uniqueness of the Jews

We learned the importance and uniqueness of the nation of Israel in the previous chapter. In this chapter, let's learn about Jews. If there is a nation, there will be its people, the citizens of that country. God, by His sovereign will and wisdom chose the Jewish people to be the citizens of the nation of Israel. First, we will establish the importance of the Jews according to Scripture. Who are Jews?

In the Bible, Jews were called Hebrews or Children of Israel. The original name for the people we now call Jews was Hebrews. The word Hebrew or Ivri is first used in the Bible to describe Abraham in Genesis 14:13, we read, "Then one who had escaped came and told Abram the Hebrew...."

The Jewish people are the descendants of Abraham, Isaac, and Jacob. The word Jew, in Hebrew, Yehudi is derived from the name Judah, which was the name of one of Jacob's twelve sons. God called Abraham from the pagan

> The original name for the people we now call Jews was Hebrews.

world and made a covenant with him. He promised to bless him and his descendants, if he would believe in the God who called him. God promised to make him a blessing to all the families of the earth. Now the LORD had said to Abram:

"Get out of your country, From your family And from your father's house, To a land that I will show you. I will make you a great nation; I will bless you And make your name great; And you shall be a blessing. I will bless those who bless you, And I will curse him who curses you; And in you all the families of the earth shall be blessed."

(Genesis 12:1-3)

## Jews Are the People of Covenant

Not only did God promise to bless Abraham, but he made a covenant with him. He made a covenant with Abraham, that through his descendants, human beings would be blessed. He made a particular covenant with his only son Isaac, whom he brought forth through his covenant wife Sarah. Then God said:

"No, Sarah your wife shall bear you a son, and you shall call his name Isaac; I will establish My covenant with him for an everlasting covenant, and with his descendants after him. And as for Ishmael, I have heard you. Behold, I have blessed him, and will make him fruitful, and will multiply him exceedingly. He shall beget twelve princes, and I will make him a great nation. But My covenant I will establish with Isaac, whom Sarah shall bear to you at this set time next year." (Genesis 17:19-21)

Here we see God clearly makes a distinction between the promised son Isaac and the son of the flesh, Ishmael, which Abraham brought forth through Hagar, the Egyptian maid. It was pure due to the impatience and unbelief of Sarah that Abraham consented to have intercourse with Hagar; as this was their cultural practices to continue one's lineage. This was clearly not God's plan, "But My covenant I will establish with Isaac, whom Sarah shall bear to you at this set time next year," as stated in Genesis 17:21.

The covenant is clear—it is only with Isaac. The Devil has been waging a big battle for thousands of years over this issue. The greatest battles are fought because of this demonic deception. Praise God, Jesus will bring an end to this chaos when He comes back to the earth.

The descendants of Abraham, Isaac, and Jacob are the Jewish people. They are the people of covenant and the land of Israel is covenanted to the Jewish people.

"And I will establish My covenant between Me and you and your descendants after you in their generation, for an everlasting covenant, to be God to you and your descendants after you in their generations, for an

covenant, to be God to you and
ıdants after you. Also I give you
:scendants after you the land in
which you are a stranger, all the land of
Canaan, as an everlasting possession; and I
will be their God." (Genesis 17:7-8)

Notice that the land of Israel is given as a possession to the Jewish people; and it is an everlasting covenant. The most amazing passage of Scripture confirming the rightful claim of the Jewish people to the land of Israel is found in the Psalm 105:6-11:

"O Seed of Abraham His servant, You children of Jacob, His chosen ones! He is the Lord our God; His judgments are in all the earth. He remembers His covenant forever, The Word which He commanded, for a thousand generations, The covenant which He made with Abraham, And His oath to Isaac, And confirmed it to Jacob for a statute, To Israel as an everlasting covenant ,

Saying, "To you I will give the land of Canaan as the allotment of your inheritance".

I don't think there is anymore need to confirm or affirm the rightful claim of the Jewish people to the land of Israel. God has done this three times in the above passage stating that Israel belongs to the Jewish people.

- First and foremost, our God is a covenant keeper; and He remembers His covenant forever.
- Secondly, if He speaks once, it is done.
- When He said, "Let there be light," the light came into existence.

In the above passage of Scripture, God made the covenant so strong by declaring it three times:

1. His **covenant** with Abraham,
2. His **oath** with Isaac, and
3. He **confirmed** it to Jacob for a statute.

Amazing! God knew the warfare that would be waged against this covenant. Therefore, He confirmed it many times in the Scripture. I think anyone denying this fact is a fanatic and insane.

Some may argue that the covenant was valid only until Jesus came—when the Jewish people did not accept Him as the Messiah, this covenant was broken. Well, Almighty God has declared it as an eternal covenant. I don't believe any force can break it.

Also, God is not a man that He can lie. Some may argue that this covenant was broken when the Jewish people disobeyed God and were scattered to all different nations. Jeremiah clears up this deception so beautifully.

"For behold the days are coming," says the Lord, "that I will bring back from captivity My people Israel and Judah," says the Lord. "And I will cause them to return to the land that I gave to their fathers, and they shall possess it." (Jeremiah 30:3)

The above passage is very clear that He will bring them back to the land He gave to their fathers, Abraham, Isaac, and Jacob. God fulfilled this promise in 1948, re-establishing Israel as a nation. He continues to bring the Jewish people from around the world to their homeland, Israel. Our God is an awesome God; and He is ever faithful.

"If the ordinances depart from before Me, says the Lord. Then the seed of Israel shall also cease from being a nation before Me forever" Jeremiah 31:36

God is not only bringing back the Jew, but has given a promise to counter the plans enemy. The enemy, through different governm leaders and organizations, is denying this fact, and try to wipe Israel off of the map of the earth. God promises to counter this plan with the following words, in Jeremiah 31:36, God declares, "If the ordinances depart from before Me, says the Lord. Then the seed of Israel shall also cease from being a nation before Me forever."

This one verse will clarify all our doubts, and also counter the fanatic and insane arguments of different demonically influenced, so called world leaders, religious leaders, and terrorist leaders. Israel belongs to the Jewish people forever, period.

## God's Chosen People Forever

In God's kingdom, every first tenth belongs to God. Christians call it the tithe. I believe God chose the Jewish people as a tithe of all the people.

> Israel belongs to the Jewish people forever.

The Bible declares that the Jewish people are the chosen people forever.

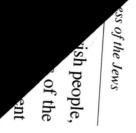

Your people, like Israel,
ne earth whom God went
self as a people, to make
e—and to do for Yourself
ne deeds for Your land—
e whom You redeemed for
Yourself from Egypt, the nations, and their
gods? For You have made Your people Israel
Your very own people forever; and You,
LORD, have become their God."

(2 Samuel 7:23-24)

Saints, this is the reason why the Jews have
been persecuted for thousands of years. They were
the chosen people to bring forth the Messiah. God
executed the plan of redemption of human beings
through them. The eternal Gospel was preached first
by the Jews to the whole world.

No wonder the devil was upset and released the
anti-semitic evil spirit to persecute this precious
chosen people for thousands of years. But sadly,
even the Church was caught up in this deception.
Praise God, now we are being delivered. Now in
these crucial end times, the evangelical Christians

around the world are the greatest supporters of the Jewish people and the nation of Israel.

## Holy People a Special Treasure

God first brought forth the principle of holiness through the Jewish people. The Scriptures describe them as the holy people and a special treasure among the people groups. Deuteronomy 7:6 reads, "For you are a holy people to the LORD your God; the LORD your God has chosen you to be a people for Himself, a special treasure above all the peoples on the face of the earth."

This is one of the reasons throughout history; the Jewish people have lived a life set apart from others. This provoked the other people in the community; and the devil used them to incite persecution against the Jews.

God is holy; and, He has called each one of us to be holy. Yet, Christians, have compromised with the world, especially in the western culture. The divorce rate is more than or equal to the world's rate. The sexual immorality is even rampant in the Churches. Instead, Western civilization should be,

"As obedient children, not conforming yourselves to the former lusts, as in your ignorance; but as He who called you is holy, you
also be holy in all your conduct, because it
is written, "Be holy, for I am holy."

(1 Peter 1:14-16)

What a wonderful life and blessing it would be
if we, as believers, washed by the precious blood
of Jesus, live a set apart life! I believe only this can
result in a worldwide revival.

**Tribe of His Inheritance:**

The Bible describes the Jewish people as God's
inheritance. In Jeremiah 10:16, we read, "The Portion
of Jacob is not like them, For He is the Maker of all
things, And Israel is the tribe of His inheritance; The
LORD of hosts is His name."

The word used for inheritance in Hebrew is
*nachalah*. This word means possession, property,
inheritance, or heritage. It means the special possession of Jehovah God, i.e. the Jewish people for

whom God cares and watches as being His own.

"For the Lord's portion is His people; Jacob is the place of His inheritance. He found him in a desert land And in the wasteland, a howling wilderness; He encircled him, He instructed him, He kept him as the apple of His eye. As an eagle stirs up its nest, Hovers over its young, Spreading out its wings, taking them up, Carrying them on its wings."

(Deuteronomy 32:9-11)

## Apple of God's Eye

Throughout history, the devil always tries to destroy the things that are very dear to the Lord. Zechariah, the prophet, writes that the Jewish people are the apple of God's eye.

"For thus says the LORD of hosts: 'He sent Me after glory, to the nations which plunder you; for he who touches you touches the apple of His eye. For surely I will shake My hand against them, and they shall become spoil for their servants. Then you will know that the LORD of hosts has sent Me.'"

(Zechariah 2:8-9)

Jewish people are not only God's inheritance, but also the apple of His eye. In this Scripture, we see a very prophetic warning for all the nations that are attacking, belittling, or persecuting Israel. We see that God will be against them and will crush them, causing them to become slaves to the devil and his agents.

"And He has exalted the horn of His people, The praise of all His saints—Of the children of Israel, A people near to Him. Praise the Lord!" (Psalm 148:14)

From the above verse it is also clear that the Jews are not only the apple of His eye, but also people near to God. Every Christian needs to hear that and make a commitment to support and bless the Jewish people.

This is the reason we see the nations, which are

40

against Israel, predominantly under the se

bondage of the spirit of
Islam. Praise God for the
Gospel! It penetrates and
sets the people free, bringing them under the bless-

> The revelation of one new man and unity between the Messianic Jews and the Gentile Christians is the key for the end time revival.

ings of Abraham, as spiritual descendants of Abraham, Isaac, and Jacob, through the blood of Jesus.

"But now in Christ Jesus you who once were far off have been brought near by the blood of Christ. For He Himself is our peace, who has made both one, and has broken down the middle wall of separation, having abolished in His flesh the enmity, that is, the law of com- mandments contained in ordinances, so as to create in Himself one new man from the two, thus making peace."

(Ephesians 2:13-15)

The revelation of one new man and unity between the Messianic Jews and the Gentile Christians is the key for the end time revival.

## uence in Dividing the Earth

zed and astonished when I first read
2:8, "When the Most High divided
their inheritance to the nations, when He separated the
sons of Adam, He set the boundaries of the peoples,
according to the number of the children of Israel."

Our God is a detailed planner to the minutest
detail. Nothing will surprise Him, as God has
planned everything eternally. He is the beginning
and the end. He is the Alpha and the Omega.

When God planned to divide the nations and set
the boundaries, He did it keeping in mind His inheritance, the children of Israel, Jewish people. Isn't this
incredible?

I would like to explain this with an illustration.
Suppose you are the father of many sons; and, you
have a huge real estate property. You are trying
to decide on how to divide it among your sons.
Prophetically, you know how many descendants will
come from your firstborn son, and you have planned
to divide your property in such a way that it will
provide all the land that they will require. Then you
divide the rest of the land among your other sons.

The Bible also teaches us that Jewish people are God's firstborn son. In Exodus 4:22, it explains, "Then you shall say to Pharaoh, 'Thus says the LORD: Israel is My son, My firstborn.'" The firstborn son gets more inheritance from his father than the other sons, in Bible times and in the culture of the Far East. We also see this in Deuteronomy 21:17.

This really amazed me. It gives such uniqueness to the Jewish people. As we know, on May 14, 1948, Israel got her independence and was re-established as a nation. Around

> When the nation of Israel is in the right place, then all nations will be aligned to their rightful places as designed by God.

the same year several other nations got their independence: India, Pakistan, Bangladesh, etc.

I believe this marked the final placement of the nations in their rightful places to usher in a worldwide revival and welcome back the King of kings to rule all the nations from Jerusalem. This was also prophesied by our Lord Jesus Himself in Luke 21:29-33:

"Then He spoke to them a parable: 'Look at the fig tree, and all the trees. When they are already budding, you see and know for yourselves that summer is now near. So you also, when you see these things happening, know that the kingdom of God is near. Assuredly, I say to you, this generation will by no means pass away till all things take place. Heaven and earth will pass away, but My words will by no means pass away.'"

We read what Jesus was saying about the fig tree blossoming and the other trees blossoming. In the Bible, the fig represents Israel. We read in Hosea 9:10, "I found Israel Like grapes in the wilderness; I saw your fathers as the first fruits on the fig tree in its first season. But they went to Baal Peor, And separated themselves to that shame; They became an abomination like the thing they loved."

What does Jesus mean by this? He meant when you see Israel become re-established and see other nations become independent (other trees), then understand that the Kingdom of God is near. He assures us that this generation will not pass away. Are we the final generation?

When we put together prophesie:
ments, we can conclude that we are
tion. Everything that is happening i
indicates that we are in the end of

May the Lord reveal to you more about the impor
tance and uniqueness of the Jewish people. May He
encourage you to have more love and compassion
for them. As you read in Psalm 102:13, "You will
arise and have mercy on Zion; For the time to favor
her, Yes, the set time, has come."

Yes, this is the set time to show mercy to the
Jewish people for all that they have gone throughout
these centuries for the sake of the nations. Will you
pray for the Jewish people? Will you bless and support them?

# Chapter Three

# The Biblical Importance and Uniqueness of Jerusalem

The city of Jerusalem is the most important city to Jehovah God and to all who fear the God of Abraham, Isaac, and Jacob. This is the city that God chose to record His name and to demonstrate His extravagant love towards the crown of His creation—human beings. Jerusalem is in the midst of the earth. In Ezekiel 5:5, it reads, "This is Jerusalem; I have set her in the midst of the nations and the countries all around her."

## The City of the Great King

The Lord Most High is the great King over all the earth. He is the great God and King above all gods.

He has chosen Jerusalem to be His city. In Matthew 5:35, Jesus declared that Jerusalem is the city of the great King, "But I say to you, do not

> Jes'
> ove.
> King of N.
> Jerusalem, the
> the great King.

swear at all: neither by heaven, for it is God's throne; nor by the earth, for it is the footstool; nor by Jerusalem, for it is the city of the great King."

Our Lord Jesus chose Jerusalem, the joy of the whole earth as His city to rule from, during His millennial reign over all the earth as the King of kings and the Lord of lords. No wonder a great battle has raged for centuries for the control over this city. The three major religions, Judaism, Christianity, and Islam believe that whoever rules Jerusalem will rule over the whole earth.

The devil and his kingdom have been completely focused on possessing control of Jerusalem. We can clearly see that the leaders of different governments and world organizations are demonically influenced and pushing man's peace process to divide Jerusalem. But, we know only God's peace process will prevail, and Jerusalem, which was covenanted to the Jewish people, will never be divided. Only the ndivided Jerusalem can usher in the coming of our Lord and Savior Jesus Christ.

In Zechariah 12:10, we read that the Jewish people will look upon Jesus and will mourn for what their religious leaders did to Him. "And I will pour on the house of David and on the inhabitants of Jerusalem the Spirit of grace and supplication; then they will look on Me whom they pierced. Yes, they will mourn for Him as one mourns for his only son, and grieve for Him as one grieves for a firstborn."

If Jerusalem is divided and the Jews are chased out, how can this Scripture be fulfilled? This clearly portrays the importance of the undivided Jerusalem to usher in the coming of our King Messiah, Jesus Christ of Nazareth. We need to stand resolute in prayer against all the forces trying to divide Jerusalem.

King David fought fearlessly over the Jebusites and won this city for the Israelites. We can read

> Only the undivided Jerusalem can usher the coming of our Lord and Savior Jesus Christ.

this conquest in 2 Samuel 5:6-10. The undivided Jerusalem, during David's reign, saw the era of greatest peace and prosperity, which continued to

Solomon's time. Jesus Christ the Son of David will reign from the undivided Jerusalem as King of kings. The whole earth will see the greatest and ultimate peace, prosperity and tranquility.

The whole creation is groaning and waiting for this awesome day. Are you ready?

## The City That Has Many Names

In the Bible days, a name signified the attributes of a person, family, place, city or a nation. It often reveals the prophetic destiny. In the Bible, the Holy Spirit has given several unique names for this city. Following are some of the names that are given to Jerusalem, which reveal her prophetic destiny.

- City of David—2 Samuel 6:10; 1 Kings 11:27; 2 Chronicles 8:11
- City of God—Psalm 46:4; Psalm 87:3
- City of Great King—Psalm 48:2; Matthew 5:35
- City of Judah—2 Chronicles 25:28
- City of God's Joy—Jeremiah 49:25
- City of the Lord – Isaiah 60:14
- City of Peace (Salem)—Hebrew 7:2

- City of Praise – Jeremiah 49:25
- City of Righteousness – Isaiah 1:26
- City of Truth—Zechariah 8:3
- Faithful City—Isaiah 1:26
- Gate of My people—Micah 1:9; Obadiah 1:13
- Green Olive Tree—Jeremiah 11:16
- Good fruit – Jeremiah 11:16
- Holy City—Nehemiah 11:1,18; Isaiah 48:2, 52:1; Daniel 9:24; Matthew 4:5; 27:53; Revelation 11:2, 21:2, 22:19
- Holy Mountain—Isaiah 11:9, 56:7; 57:13, 65:25; 66:20; Ezekiel 20:40; Daniel 9:16, 20; Joel 2:1, 3:17; Zephaniah 3:11; Zechariah 8:3
- Lovely – Jeremiah 11:16
- Mountain of the Lord of Hosts – Zechariah 8:3
- Throne of the Lord—Jeremiah 3:17
- Zion—1 Kings 8:1; Isaiah 60:14; Zechariah 9:13

Amazing! Jerusalem is a city of many names. As you observe, most of them will be fulfilled during the millennial rule of Jesus Christ.

## Jerusalem - A City of Destiny

Jerusalem is mentioned approximately 822 times in the New King James Version of the Bible and 1035 times in the New Living Translation. It is a unique city, both in the world and in the heart of our God.

In 2 Chronicles 6:6, let us read, "Yet I have chosen Jerusalem, that My name may be there, and I have chosen David to be over My people Israel." The creator of heaven and earth chose this city to put His Name. I encourage you to pray and keep this city of your God dear to your heart.

## God's Dwelling Place

In Psalm 132:13-14, it reads, "For the LORD has chosen Zion; He has desired it for His dwelling place: "This is My resting place forever; Here I will dwell, for I have desired it." It's amazing to know the fact that our God has chosen Mt. Zion in Jerusalem as His desired dwelling place. It is His resting place forever.

When, ultimately, Jesus destroys the enemies of God and rests in Jerusalem, the whole world will be ushered into an age of peace and harmony as described in Isaiah. And you will know, as told in Joel 3:17,"So you shall know that I am the LORD your God, Dwelling in Zion My holy mountain…."

Also, it is interesting to note that David got the revelation from God that Jerusalem is His resting place. He tirelessly worked to provide for the temple that his son Solomon would build. In Psalm 132:4-5, David writes, "I will not give sleep to my eyes Or slumber to my eyelids, Until I find a place for the Lord, A dwelling place for the Mighty one of Jacob."

No wonder the Shekinah Glory of God manifested in a tangible way in the temple. Are we relentlessly praying and working for the salvation of the Jews and all the nations which will bring the true lasting peace to the world under the Kingship of the Prince of Peace? The prophet Ezekiel had the same revelation as David. But Ezekiel's revelation is yet to be fulfilled and will be fulfilled during the millennial reign of our Lord Jesus Christ.

"The Spirit lifted me up and brought me into the inner court; and behold, the glory of the LORD filled the temple. Then I heard Him speaking to me from the temple, while a man stood beside me. And He said to me, 'Son of man, this is the place of My throne and the place of the soles of My feet, where I will dwell in the midst of the children of Israel forever. No more shall the house of Israel defile My holy name, they nor their kings, by their harlotry or with the carcasses of their kings on their high places.'" (Ezekiel 43:5-7)

Jesus the Christ will be enthroned on His throne in the temple. The soles of His feet will be standing in Jerusalem. He will dwell in the midst of the children of Israel forever. What an awesome privilege the Jewish people have! They are going through all these persecutions for thousands of years, due to this glorious calling on them.

## Eastern or Golden Gate

Jerusalem is the city where a closed gate still stands waiting for the fulfillment of the prophesy for Jesus to walk right through it.

"Afterward he brought me to the gate, the gate that faces toward the east. And behold, the glory of the God of Israel came from the way of east. His voice was like the sound of many waters; and the earth shone with His glory. And the glory of the Lord came into the temple by the way of the gate which faces toward the east." (Ezekiel 43:1,2 & 4)

The Eastern Gate, or Golden Gate, is the oldest of the city gates and is located along the eastern wall of the Temple Mount. On Palm Sunday, Jesus rode into the city through the Eastern Gate. We believe the Eastern Gate, which has been sealed for many centuries, will reopen upon the return of Christ.

"Then He brought me back to the outer gate of the sanctuary which faces toward the east, but it was shut. And the LORD said to me, "This gate shall be shut; it shall not be opened, and no man shall enter by it, because the LORD God of Israel has entered by it; therefore it shall be shut." (Ezekiel 44:1-2)

The Golden Gate, as it is called in Christian literature and in Jewish tradition, is the gate where the Shekinah, divine presence, used to appear; and it will appear again when the Messiah comes, as written in Ezekiel 44:1–3. Also, note that in Arabic, it is known as the Gate of Eternal Life.

In Jewish tradition, this is the gate through which the Messiah will enter Jerusalem. Ottoman Sultan Suleiman I sealed off the Golden Gate in 1541 to prevent the Messiah's entrance. It is regarded as a Holy site for three major faiths: Judaism (arrival of the Messiah), Christianity (entrance of Jesus on Palm Sunday and also in His second coming), and Islam (site of future resurrection).

Jerusalem is a city of destiny, be on watch and

pray for its peace. Pray that the Jewish people will be delivered from their blindness and receive the Messiah.

## A City No One Should Forget

We read in Psalm 137:5-6, the lamentations of the Jews during the Babylonian captivity. Individually the captives pledge their fidelity to Jerusalem. "If I forget you, O Jerusalem, Let my right hand forget its skill! If I do not remember you, Let my tongue cling to the roof of my mouth—If I do not exalt Jerusalem above my chief joy."

Israelites were ready to give up anything, including their very gifts and abilities of its livelihood. Are Christians showing the same fidelity to Jerusalem, where our Savior was crucified on the cross for each one of our sins, and where He will rule from as King of kings and Lord of lords?

I encourage you to pray and take a stand for Jerusalem; because, it is still very close to God's heart. In its peace, lies the peace of the whole earth. Align yourself with God's heart and His sight. Begin to show compassion for Israel's current condition.

In Psalm 102:13-14, "You will arise and have mercy on Zion; For the time to favor her, Yes, the set time, has come. For Your servants take pleasure in her stones, And show favor to her dust."

In Psalm 51:18, you are commanded to do good to Jerusalem, "Do good in Your good pleasure to Zion; Build the walls of Jerusalem."

In Psalm 51:17, you are told that God does not despise the broken spirit and a contrite heart. "The sacrifices of God are a broken spirit, A broken and a contrite heart—These, O God, You will not despise."

He adds, in Psalm 51:19, that when you do good to Jerusalem, you are actually offering sacrifices of righteousness; and God is pleased. "Then You shall be pleased with the sacrifices of righteousness."

Take an effort to bless Jerusalem. Do something good to her people; and see your own prayers answered.

## The City of the Appointed Feasts

God has appointed seven feasts for the Jewish people to observe. In Leviticus 23:2, it reads, "Speak to the children of Israel, and say to them: 'The feasts of the LORD, which you shall proclaim to be holy convocations, these are My feasts.'"

Following the fall of man in the Garden of Eden, the Feasts were given to us by God so His people could understand the coming of the Messiah and the role the Messiah would play to redeem and restore both man and the earth back to God. They are shadows of the coming things and point towards the Messiah, Jesus Christ. Every feast is fulfilled in Jesus Christ. In Colossians 2:16-17, it reads, "So let no one judge you in food or in drink, or regarding a festival or a new moon or sabbaths, which are a shadow of things to come, but the substance is of Christ."

The first four feasts were fulfilled in the first

coming of our Lord Jesus Christ. Every minute detail is fulfilled exactly in the death, burial, and resurrection of Jesus Christ.

1. The Passover (Crucifixion and death of Jesus Christ the Messiah)
2. Unleavened Bread (Burial of Jesus the Messiah)
3. The Feast of the Firstfruits (Resurrection of Jesus Christ)
4. The Feast of the Weeks or Pentecost (Coming of the Holy Spirit on the Pentecost)

The following three feasts will be fulfilled, during the rapture, tribulation, and millennial reign of Jesus Christ.

5. The Feast of Trumpets (Rapture or catching up of the Church. 1 Corinthians 15:51-52; 1 Thessalonians 4:16-17).
6. The Day of Atonement (Tribulation)
7. The Feast of Tabernacles (Millennial reign of Jesus Christ the Messiah)

God has also appointed the right place to keep these feasts. It is Jerusalem; the city of the great

King. The city that God has chosen to put His Name on. (Deuteronomy 16:2, 6, 11 and 2 Kings 21:4)

"Look upon Zion, the city of our appointed feasts; Your eyes will see Jerusalem, a quiet home, A tabernacle that will not be taken down; Not one of its stakes will ever be removed, Nor will any of its cords be broken"

(Isaiah 33:20)

## City from Where the Blessings Flow

God has commanded His blessings on Mount Zion in Jerusalem. "It is like the dew of Hermon, Descending upon the mountains of Zion; For there the LORD commanded the blessing—Life forevermore" Psalm 133:3.

This is the testimony of the millions who visited Jerusalem. They were blessed as they truly worshipped the Lord in Jerusalem. God has commanded His blessings there.

Also in the above Scripture, God commanded life forevermore, which is eternal life. It was in Jerusalem that Jesus redeemed us through His precious blood;

He bought us eternal life. Truly there is an eternal blessing resting upon Jerusalem.

## City of Prophetic Fulfillment

Jerusalem is the city where many prophetic promises were fulfilled and are, yet to be fulfilled. Jerusalem is a city of destiny. Following are a few important occurrences that are so dear to our faith in fulfilling many of the Biblical prophesies. Jerusalem is the city where:

- The first and the second Temple stood
- The Shekinah Glory manifested in the temple
- The people witnessed the greatest demonstration of love that saves the whole human race, the crucifixion of Jesus Christ
- Jesus resurrected from the Garden Tomb
- The Holy Spirit first came upon the Jews during the Pentecost
- The first Church began
- The Gospel went out to the ends of the earth
- All nations will gather against before the coming of the Lord

- Jesus will land back on Mount of Olives in Jerusalem
- Jesus will rule from Mount Zion, Jerusalem
- Earthly Jerusalem will be replaced by the Heavenly Jerusalem

## The City Whose Architect is God Himself

This is the city that God Himself designed and built; all the patriarchs went and built altars and worshipped our God there. In fact, Abraham left the Chaldeans in faith and walked all the way, trusting to see this magnificent city of destiny.

"By faith Abraham obeyed when he was called to go out to the place which he would receive as an inheritance. And he went out, not knowing where he was going. By faith he dwelt in the land of promise as in a foreign country, dwelling in tents with Isaac and Jacob, the heirs with him of the same promise; for he waited for the city which has foundations, whose builder and maker is God."

(Hebrews 11:8-10)

As we go to Israel and walk in the streets of Jerusalem, we can feel the presence of God. There is an incredible difference from any other city in the world. God regards this city very much; we as His children, should regard this city as well. We understand the significance is due to her builder and architect, who is God Himself.

God is not only its architect; but, He is also its defender. There have been several conquests and battles over this city to destroy it and its people. No one can ultimately succeed as God Himself defends it. In 2 Kings 19:34, we read, "For I will defend this city, to save it For My own sake and for My servant David's sake."

God not only defends Jerusalem, He restored it back to the Jewish people during the Yom Kippur war in 1967. It was just another supernatural victory for the Jews and

> Jerusalem is a city that will abide from generation to generation.

this city. Our God is faithful; His words are ever settled in heavens. No matter how hard the devil tries and all nations come against her, the Word of the Lord is very clear that Jerusalem will stand forever. In Joel 3:20, we read, "But Judah shall abide forever

And Jerusalem from generation to generation."

## The City That is Awaiting the Arrival of Jesus Christ

One city in the entire world that is waiting for the arrival of Jesus Christ is Jerusalem. Though it doesn't look like it in the natural, spiritually, an end time revival is around the corner. The Mount of Olives is getting ready for the landing of Jesus' feet. What an awesome day it will be when King of kings returns back with all the believers to reign from Jerusalem!

"On that day his feet will stand on the Mount of Olives, which faces Jerusalem on the east. And the Mount of Olives will split apart, making a wide valley running from east to west, for half the mountain will move toward the north and half toward the south." (Zechariah 14:4)

While I was living in Israel, I was living right on the Mount of Olives. I used to tell my kids and make fun, "If Jesus comes tonight, He will be landing right on our home. We will be the first ones to see in the whole world." Even that thought brings a chill on my spine. Glorious days are ahead for the heavily despised Jerusalem.

## The City Every Nation Will Be Offended by:

Every nation will be offended by Jerusalem in the end times. Zechariah describes it as being like a heavy stone for those who reject God's plan of redemption and neglect the gospel. It will be a time of delusion and complete deception on part of the nations.

"The burden of the Word of the LORD against Israel. Thus says the LORD, who stretches out the heavens, lays the foundation of the earth, and forms the spirit of man within him: 'Behold, I will make Jerusalem a cup of drunkenness to all the surrounding peoples, when they lay siege against Judah and Jerusalem.' And it shall happen in that day that I will make Jerusalem a very heavy stone for all peoples; all who would heave it away will surely be cut in pieces, though all nations of the earth are gathered against it."

(Zechariah 12:1-3)

We see this happening right in front of our eyes. Many nations are aligning according to the end time prophesies and getting ready to fight Jerusalem.

"For I will gather all the nations to battle against Jerusalem; The city shall be taken, The houses rifled, And the women ravished. Half of the city shall go into captivity, But the remnant of the people shall not be cut off from the city. Then the LORD will go forth And fight against those nations, As He fights in the day of battle." (Zechariah 14:2-3)

No matter how hard the nations tried to defeat Jerusalem and annihilate the Jews,

> No matter how hard the nations try to defeat Jerusalem and annihilate the Jews, God always comes to her rescue.

God always comes to her rescue. This time Jesus Christ, Himself, will come and defend her, destroy all His enemies, and establish the millennial rule.

"Now I saw heaven opened, and behold, a white horse. And He who sat on him was called Faithful and True, and in righteousness He judges and makes war. His eyes were like a flame of fire, and on His head were many crowns. He had a name written that no one knew except Himself. He was clothed with a robe dipped in blood, and His name is called The Word of God. And the armies in heaven, clothed in fine linen, white and clean, followed Him on white horses. Now out of His mouth goes a sharp sword, that with it He should strike the nations. And He Himself will rule them with a rod of iron. He Himself treads the winepress of the fierceness and wrath of Almighty God. And He has on His robe and on His thigh a name written: KING OF KINGS AND LORD OF LORDS."

(Revelation 19:11-16)

Let us stand resolute in support of Israel in these end times to usher in the coming of the Lord. May the revelation and impartation of the importance of

Jerusalem come upon the body of Christ in these end times. "Even so, come, Lord Jesus" as it reads in Revelation 22:20.

# Chapter Four

# Why Should We Pray for the Peace of Jerusalem?

"Pray for the peace of Jerusalem: 'May they prosper who love you. Peace be within your walls, Prosperity within your palaces.'"

(Psalm 122:6-7)

Many of us know this Scripture by heart. In fact, scores of Christians have made this a daily prayer in order to be prosperous.

- But do we know the real magnitude of this Scripture?
- How dear is it to our Father?

- How does it really affect the coming of the Lord?

In the following pages, we will explore together the underlying spiritual truths in the above Scripture. "Pray for the peace of Jerusalem" is a command by our Father to every Bible believing Jew and Gentile. The God of heaven and earth seeks the peace of this city. In its peace, lies the peace of the whole world. There will be true peace in the world, only when there is true peace prevailing in Jerusalem, the city of the great King.

## Jerusalem, the City of the Great King

"But I say to you, do not swear at all: neither by heaven, for it is God's throne; nor by the earth, for it is His footstool; nor by Jerusalem, for it is the city of the great King." (Matthew 5:34-35)

Jerusalem is the city where heaven and earth meets. Jesus explains that heaven is the throne of God; and the earth is His foot stool. Jerusalem is the city where He will stand with His

| Jerusalem is the city of the Great King Jesus Christ |
| --- |

authority as the King of kings and Lord of rule the whole world during His millennial re

There will not be true peace until Jesus comes. Every other process that does not involve the Jewish Messiah, our Savior Jesus Christ, will not prosper. It is meaningless to think of a solution to the problem in the Middle East, which began in Abraham's time, without the intervention of the God of Abraham, Isaac and Jacob, the God of Israel.

Both the Jewish people and the nations ignore the One who built this city. We read in the previous chapter that God Himself is the builder and architect of Jerusalem, as noted in Hebrews 11:8-10. Every peace process that has been initiated by the United States of America, United Nations, and other nations is either demonically inspired or politically moti-vated to gain control of Jerusalem.

We are commanded by God to pray for the peace of Jerusalem. When we pray for the peace of Jerusalem, we are praying for the second

> We hasten the coming of the Lord.

coming of Jesus Christ. We hasten the coming of the Lord.

In the following paragraphs, we will explore how

.y for the peace of Jerusalem to

**Condition for Jesus to**

There is a protocol for every King or a President to visit a place. Jesus our King has mentioned the protocol for Him to come back, in Matthew 23:39. "For I say to you, you shall see Me no more till you say, 'Blessed is He who comes in the name of the LORD!'"

It is very plain and clear, in order for Him to come back, the people whom He has seen already must

> There will be true peace in the world only when the Prince of Peace comes back and rules from Jerusalem.

proclaim "Blessed is He who comes in the name of the Lord." We know from this Scripture that Jesus is addressing His Jewish disciples. So Jesus declares that until the Jewish people declare Psalm 118:26, He cannot come back; and they cannot see Him again.

Here the Hebrew word for blessed is barak. Barak means to be adored, to praise, salute or to cause to kneel. When the Jewish people understand that Jesus is the true Messiah, bless Him, and kneel before Him, then all nations will bow before Him. Hallelujah!

"Therefore God also has highly exalted Him and given Him the name which is above every name, that at the name of Jesus every knee should bow, of those in heaven, and of those on earth, and of those under the earth, and [that] every tongue should confess that Jesus Christ is Lord, to the glory of God the Father."

(Philippians 2:9-11)

How will the Jewish people bless Jesus, unless they are born again and accept Him as their Lord and Savior? So, the bottom line is that Jewish people must be saved. This is the number one condition for His coming back. "And so all Israel will be saved," as stated in Romans 11:26.

This is what the LORD says: "Just as the heavens cannot be measured and the foundations of the earth cannot be explored, so I will not consider casting them away for the evil they have done. I, the LORD, have spoken. Jeremiah 31; 37 NLT

Many of the Christians believe that God was

done with the Jewish people, when they rejected Him during His first coming. Christians believe that because of the rejection and crucifixion of Jesus by the Jewish religious leaders, cooperating with the Roman Empire, God was done with them. Peter explains this clearly and defends the Jewish people, during his sermon on Solomon's porch, in Acts 3:13-15.

> "The God of Abraham, Isaac, and Jacob, the God of our fathers, glorified His Servant Jesus, whom you delivered up and denied in the presence of Pilate, when he was determined to let Him go. 'But you denied the Holy One and the Just, and asked for a murderer to be granted to you, "and killed the Prince of life, whom God raised from the dead, of which we are witnesses.'"

Although the Jews rejected their own Messiah, Peter explains that it all happened according to the plan of God.

"Yet now, brethren, I know that you did it in ignorance, as did also your rulers. 'But those things which God foretold by the mouth of all His prophets, that the Christ would suffer, He has thus fulfilled.'" (Acts 3:17-18)

God has ordained the dispensations according to His divine calendar. Everything works towards the redemption of the human race. Even Jesus Himself forgave the religious leaders who crucified Him on the cross and then asked the Father to

> "For the LORD will not forsake His people, for His great name's sake, because it has pleased the LORD to make you His people." (1 Samuel 12:22)

forgive them. In Luke 23:34, it reads, "Then Jesus said, 'Father, forgive them, for they do not know what they do....'"

Everything that happened, happened for the redemption of the human race. Jews were the chosen people to accomplish this. As noted in Romans 9:11, "for the children not yet being born, nor having done any good or evil, that the purpose of God according to election might stand, not of works but of Him who calls."

Because of the ignorance and deception, many believe that Israel and the Jewish people are replaced by the Church. They think there are no more people of promise, all of the covenants and promises are now transferred to the Christians and the Church.

This is what is called 'Replacement Theology.' There is no scriptural validity for this. It is demonically influenced and supported by many pastors and leaders, due to their lack of scriptural knowledge. Our God is an unchanging God—His promises will never change. In fact, the devil uses this theology to stop the blessings that will come, when believers support and pray for the salvation of the Jewish people.

Jewish people are a separate entity and the Church is a separate entity. Both are chosen people to God; and, they will converge at the end times. In fact, the Jewish people will proclaim the Gospel throughout the whole world in the end times. There is a give and take between the Jews and the Gentile Church. God by His divine wisdom has kept the Church to receive certain things from the Jews; and, the Jews

> Jews and Christians are chosen people to God; and, they will converge at the end times.

will have to receive from the Church in certain other areas. God's fullness of the plan will be worked out through the unity of the One New Man in Christ Jesus, the Jews and Gentiles through the blood of Yeshua as one body.

I personally believe that God chose the Jewish people to bring the revelation of the Jehovah God, His Son Jesus Christ and the redemption plan to the human race. Look at Romans 9:4-5, "who are Israelites, to whom pertain the adoption, the glory, the covenants, the giving of the law, the service of God, and the promises; of whom are the fathers and from whom, according to the flesh, Christ came, who is over all, the eternally blessed God. Amen."

From the birthing of the Church, God chose the believers in Jesus to bring the revelation of the outpouring of the Holy Spirit, the preaching of the gospel to the world, the ministry of the Holy Spirit, and the rapture of the Church. Following is the combined version of Mark 16:15-18; Matthew 28:19-20 and Luke 24:47-49 to give more clarity to the role of the Church.

"And He said to them 'Go into all the world and preach the gospel to every creature...' and that repentance and remission of sins should be preached in His name to all nations, beginning at Jerusalem.... He who believes and is baptized will be saved; but he who does not believe will be condemned.... And you are witnesses of these things.... Go therefore and make disciples of all the nations, baptizing them in the name of the Father and of the Son and of the Holy Spirit, teaching them to observe all things that I have commanded you.... Behold, I send the Promise of My Father upon you; but tarry in the city of Jerusalem until you are endued with power from on high.... And these signs will follow those who believe: In My name they will cast out demons; they will speak with new tongues; they will take up serpents; and if they drink anything deadly, it will by no means hurt them; they will lay hands on the sick, and they will recover.... And this gospel of the kingdom will be preached in all the world as a witness to all the nations, and then the end will come."

Again the Jewish people will play a major role in preaching the gospel during the tribulation, culminating in the end of the age, and the second coming of our Lord Jesus Christ. Isaiah has prophesied this; and, we will see its fulfillment as described in the book of Revelation.

> "Indeed He says, 'It is too small a thing that You should be My Servant To raise up the tribes of Jacob, And to restore the preserved ones of Israel; I will also give You as a light to the Gentiles, That You should be My salvation to the ends of the earth.'" (Isaiah 49:6)

Many students of the Bible Prophecy and Bible Scholars believe that the 12,000 from each tribe of Israel, a total of 144,000, will be supernaturally sealed and protected by God. They are called the "first fruits to God and the lamb," noted in Revelation 7:4-8. They will preach the Gospel during the tribulation and multitudes will come to the Kingdom.

> "Then I looked, and behold, a Lamb standing on Mount Zion, and with Him one hundred

and forty-four thousand, having His Father's name written on their foreheads. These are the ones who were not defiled with women, for they are virgins. These are the ones who follow the Lamb wherever He goes. These were redeemed from among men, being first-fruits to God and to the Lamb."

(Revelation 14:1 and 4)

So, it is a combined package to accomplish the redemptive plan of our awesome God, using His chosen people, the Jews and the Church. Also, when the Church recognizes her Jewish root, it will result in the fullness of the Church and the salvation of the Jews.

To further establish that the Jews or the nation of Israel is not replaced by the Church, let us consider the following principle from the Scriptures. The Bible declares that anything will be established by two or three witnesses, in 2 Corinthians 13:1, "By the mouth of two or three witnesses every word shall be established," and in Deuteronomy 19:15, "by the mouth of two or three witnesses the matter shall be established."

Our God is establishing by two wi[...] Jewish people and the Church, that He is [...] ator of everything; and, His Son is the Savior o[...] world through the power of His Holy Spirit. Also, th[...] people who lived and served our Jehovah God before Abraham like Adam, Enoch, and Noah are the third witnesses. They lived before the call of Abraham, the Hebrew, and before God chose the descendants of Abraham, Isaac, and Jacob as the chosen people.

Praise to the Lord! God is opening up the eyes of the Christians; and, many are now standing in support of Israel and the Jewish people. We must pray for the salvation of the Jewish people. God has opened the eyes of many pastors, leaders, and believers. Many Church movements are actively engaged in prayer and support of Israel. In fact, Evangelical Christians are the largest supporters of Israel in these end times.

## All Israel Will Be Saved

We understand the number one condition for the coming back of our Lord Jesus is the salvation of the Jewish people. God is doing a mighty work among the Jewish people; and many are coming to Lord.

h, Messianic Congregations
in Israel. In Israel, almost
ievers and congregations. It
)rthodox Jewish people are

ɪ ᴏʀ I do not desire, brethren, that you should
be ignorant of this mystery, lest you should be
wise in your own opinion, that blindness in
part has happened to Israel until the fullness
of the Gentiles has come in. And so all Israel
will be saved, as it is written: 'The Deliverer
will come out of Zion, And He will turn away
ungodliness from Jacob.'" (Romans 11:25-26)

Paul clearly confronts the Church's opinion that
we have replaced the Jewish people. Many Christians
are ignorant. He explains that a spiritual blindness
has happened to Israel for a purpose and a reason.
Before I explain the purpose, I would attempt to
explain what Paul meant when he wrote "And so all
Israel will be saved."

Here, "all Israel" does not necessarily mean every
Jewish person on the planet earth; rather it refers to

the remnant of the Jewish people, who will call upon the Lord. As we read in Isaiah 10:22-23, it brings more clarity to this as Paul quotes it in Romans 9:27-28, "Isaiah also cries out concerning Israel: "Though the number of the children of Israel be as the sand of the sea, The remnant will be saved. For He will finish the work and cut it short in righteousness, Because the LORD will make a short work upon the earth.""

Paul validates this again in Romans 11:1 He explains that Israel's rejection is not total and God was not done with them. "I say then, has God cast away His people? Certainly not! For I also am an Israelite, of the seed of Abraham, of the tribe of Benjamin. God has not cast away His people whom He foreknew…."

Further, Paul explains this referring to what Elijah was ignorant of. We can draw a parallel with this to our present day Church's ignorance of the remnant of the Jewish people. The following Scripture can further enlighten our understanding:

"God has not cast away His people whom He foreknew. Or do you not know what the Scripture says of Elijah, how he pleads with God against Israel, saying, "LORD, they have killed Your prophets and torn down Your altars, and I alone am left, and they seek my life?" (Romans 11:2,3)

But what does the divine response say to him? "I have reserved for Myself seven thousand men who have not bowed the knee to Baal."

(Romans 11:4)

"Even so then, at this present time there is a remnant according to the election of grace."

(Romans 11:5)

"...And so all Israel will be saved, as it is written: 'The Deliverer will come out of Zion, And He will turn away ungodliness from Jacob.'" (Romans 11:25-26)

The salvation of this remnant of the Jewish people will bring the world-wide revival ushering in the rapture of the Church. Before that, I would like to explain why they have not received the gospel; and, their eyes were blinded to receive Jesus as their Messiah. It is because of their stumbling and blindness that the salvation has come to the Gentiles.

"I say then, have they stumbled that they should fall? Certainly not! But through their fall, to provoke them to jealousy, salvation has come to the Gentiles. Now if their fall is riches for the world, and their failure riches for the Gentiles, how much more their fullness!" (Romans 11:11-12)

How long will this stumbling and blindness be? It all depends on you and me, and the extent of the Church's involvement in the worldwide evangelistic effort. Paul explains in the book of Romans.

"For I do not desire, brethren, that you should be ignorant of this mystery, lest you should be wise in your own opinion, that blindness in part has happened to Israel until the fullness of the Gentiles has come in."

(Romans 11:25)

85

For right now, Israel has not obtained the salvation but the Gentiles, once the fullness of the Gentiles have come into the Kingdom of God then all Israel will be saved.

"What then? Israel has not obtained what it seeks; but the elect have obtained it, and the rest were blinded." (Romans 11:7)

But when they receive the salvation it will usher in an unprecedented worldwide revival and the rapture of the Church.

"For if their being cast away is the reconciling of the world, what will their acceptance be but life from the dead?" (Romans 11:15)

When the Church honors and recognizes her Jewish roots, it will result in the fullness of the Church and the Jewish salvation. This will trigger the fullness of the One New Man culminating into to worldwide revival and usher in the rapture.

When we pray for the peace of Jerusalem, we are praying for the salvation of the Jewish people.

As we pray for the peace of Jerusalem, we are praying for the salvation of the Jewish people. Unless the Jewish people are saved, the condition for His return, as mentioned by Jesus himself in Matthew 23:39, will not happen.

## The Harvest of the Nations

Please understand, that a higher rate of salvation of the Jewish people will not happen, until the fullness of the Gentiles comes into the Kingdom of God. In Romans 11:25, we read, "For I do not desire, brethren, that you should be ignorant of this mystery, lest you should be wise in your own opinion, that blindness in part has happened to Israel until the fullness of the Gentiles has come in."

Every Gentile soul destined to eternal life must be saved before all the remnant of Israel gets saved. So when we pray for the peace of Jerusalem, we are also praying for the harvest of the nations, the Gentiles. The Gospel of the Kingdom will

> When we pray for the peace of Jerusalem, it actually accelerates the evangelism thrust.

be preached to all nations; and then, the end will

come. Unless the Gospel is preached, how can people hear and receive Jesus as their Savior.

It is interesting to note that when we pray for the peace of Jerusalem, it actually accelerates the evangelism thrust. Let's look to God, in Isaiah 45:21,22, "...There is no other God besides Me, A just God and a Savior; There is none besides Me. Look to Me, and be saved, All you ends of the earth! For I am God, and there is no other."

I have heard many testimonies about Churches and Ministries, who give importance to pray for the peace of Jerusalem, reach out to the lost in a higher level and continue to grow. Their ministries exploded, when they got the revelation about praying for the peace of Jerusalem and implemented it in their churches and ministries. I believe an anointing is released to reach the lost, when we pray for the peace of Jerusalem, along with the reward and blessings this anointing carries.

The gospel went from Jerusalem to the end of the earth, covering all the nations. But now, the gospel is triumphing from the end of the earth, through all nations back to Jerusalem. Surely this will usher in a great end time revival in Israel, the rapture, or taking away of the Church, and finally culminate into the end of the age. (1 Thessalonians 4:16-18; 1 Corinthians 15:52)

## Salvation of the Ishmaels and Muslims:

Our God is a righteous judge and a merciful God. He is full of compassion; and He is not willing that even a single soul should perish, 2 Peter 3:9. God did not forget the Ishmaels or the Arabs. Ishmael was

> When we pray for the peace of Jerusalem we are praying for the harvest of the nations.

born to Abraham through Hagar, the handmaiden of Sarah. Although the covenant was only with Isaac, God did promise that the descendants of Ishmael would be blessed and increase.

Ishmael had 12 sons, who became the founders of Ishmaelite tribes that spread from Egypt to Iraq and the adjoining territories. The overwhelming majority of them are Muslims. God has promised this group of people will be saved through the blood of Jesus; and, they will worship the Lord along with the Jewish people, as a blessing in the midst of the earth.

89

"In that day there will be a highway from Egypt to Assyria, and the Assyrian will come into Egypt and the Egyptian into Assyria, and the Egyptians will serve with the Assyrians. In that day Israel will be one of three with Egypt and Assyria—a blessing in the midst of the land, whom the LORD of hosts shall bless, saying, 'Blessed is Egypt My people, and Assyria the work of My hands, and Israel My inheritance.'" (Isaiah 19:23-25)

God is breaking the middle wall of separation through the blood of Jesus—The One New Man is breaking through. While living in Israel, I witnessed this prophecy literally come to pass. Jewish and Arab believers are worshiping the God of Abraham, our Lord Jesus Christ, together. We are going to see the fullness of this prophecy come to pass in our generation. As we pray for the peace of Jerusalem, we are praying for the salvation of the Arabs and the Muslims.

I encourage you to pray for the peace of Jerusalem with this understanding. You are called to love your Muslim brothers and sisters. You need to love your Arab brethren. God sent His only begotten Son to die for the whole world. As you pray and spread the love of Christ, I believe the Muslims and Arabs will come to the Lord at a higher rate. When you pray God is going to do a quick work to bring the fullness of the above prophecy.

## Re-gathering of the Jewish People:

The salvation of all the remnant of the Jewish people is the primary fulfillment before the heaven releases Jesus Christ back to the earth. We read, in Acts 3:20-21, "...and that He may send Jesus Christ, who was preached to you before whom heaven must receive until the times of restoration of all things, which God has spoken by the mouth of all His holy prophets since the world began."

The temple was destroyed and the Jewish people were scattered all over the world. Jesus prophesied this; and then, it happened around 70 AD.

"And Jesus said to them, 'Do you not see all these things? Assuredly, I say to you, not one stone shall be left here upon another, that shall not be thrown down.'" (Matthew 24:2)

"And they will fall by the edge of the sword, and be led away captive into all nations. And Jerusalem will be trampled by Gentiles until the times of the Gentiles are fulfilled."

(Luke 21:24)

The Jewish people were scattered all over the earth, due to their disobedience to God and His covenant. In the book of Deuteronomy 28, God promised blessings that would come upon them when they obey the Lord. He also warned that curses would come upon and overtake them, and they would be scattered all over the world, when they disobey.

"You shall be left few in number, whereas you were as the stars of heaven in multitude, because you would not obey the voice of the LORD your God.... Then the LORD will scatter you among all peoples, from one end of the earth to the other, and there.... And among those nations you shall find no rest, nor shall the sole of your foot have a resting place...." (Deuteronomy 28:62-68)

God also warned, time and time again, through His prophets that disaster would come upon them; and, they would be scattered among the nations, if they continued to disobey Him.

"But this is what I commanded them, saying, 'Obey My voice, and I will be your God.... Yet they did not obey or incline their ear, but followed the counsels and the dictates of their evil hearts.... Since the day that your fathers came out of the land of Egypt until this day, I have even sent to you all My servants the prophets, daily rising up early and sending them. 'Yet they did not obey Me or incline their ear....' They did worse than their fathers." Jeremiah 7: 23-26

Our God is a righteous God. His Words are ever settled in heavens. According to His Word, the Jewish people continued to drift away from Him. Over the score of many centuries, they were systematically scattered all

> "I will scatter you among the nations and draw out a sword after you; your land shall be desolate and your cities waste." (Leviticus 26:33)

over the world, ridiculed, and persecuted.

I just want to reiterate that Christians serve the same God. It is imperative that we obey the Lord our Savior; and, do what He is calling us to do. This will bring blessings into our lives. Many Christians do not understand that they open themselves up to curses, when they do not obey His voice.

Jesus said that His sheep will hear His voice. The most important requirement for His children is to continuously hear the voice of God and obey Him. Be not only hearers, but the doers of the Word. It is a mandatory requirement and not an option.

Though the Jewish people were scattered, yet God by His mercy and grace prophesied through His holy prophets in over 600 Scriptures that He will bring the Jewish people back to the land of Israel.

"'For a mere moment I have forsaken you, But with great mercies I will gather you. With a little wrath I hid My face from you for a moment; But with everlasting kindness I will have mercy on you,' Says the LORD, your Redeemer." (Isaiah 54:7-8)

In Hebrew, the re-gathering of the Jewish people or the immigration of the Jewish people back to the land of Israel is called, 'Aliyah'. It is translated as ascent—this is the immigration to the Land of Israel by the Jewish people. Ezekiel prophesied that the Jewish people will receive Jesus as their Messiah in a wider scale, when they are gathered back to the land of Israel. Ezekiel 36 gives a step by step redemption of the Jewish people to their land and to their Messiah. First they will be gathered back to their land.

"For I will take you from among the nations, gather you out of all countries, and bring you into your own land." (Ezekiel 36:24)

Once the re-gathering happens, then He will use His Jewish and Gentile believers to preach the gospel to the Jewish people in the land of Israel. I believe it is predominately done by the Jewish believers and their congregations.

"Then I will sprinkle clean water on you, and you shall be clean; I will cleanse you from all your filthiness and from all your idols."

(Ezekiel 36:25)

Here the sprinkling of water is the typology for the preaching of the Word, as we read in Ephesians 5:26. As we read on in Ezekiel, we see the progress; God will give them a new heart and a new Spirit, the Holy Spirit, to receive the New Covenant through the Messiah Jesus Christ. Once their heart is renewed, they will be filled with the Holy Spirit to cause them to walk in His statutes.

"I will give you a new heart and put a new spirit within you; I will take the heart of stone out of your flesh and give you a heart of flesh. I will put My Spirit within you and cause you to walk in My statutes, and you will keep My judgments and do them." (Ezekiel 36:25-27)

Once they receive their Messiah, then they are assured the complete governance of the land of Israel.

"Then you shall dwell in the land that I gave to your fathers; you shall be My people, and I will be your God." (Ezekiel 24:28)

After 1900 plus years of absence in the land of Israel, God began to slowly bring back the Jewish people. God did a miraculous work; and, in a single day, He reestablished the Jewish state of Israel on May 14, 1948.

> "Therefore say, 'Thus says the Lord GOD: I will gather you from the peoples, assemble you from the countries where you have been scattered, and I will give you the land of Israel.'" (Ezekiel 11:17)

The prophecy in Isaiah 66:8 was fulfilled in front of the eyes of this generation. This is a tremendous testimony for the faithfulness of our God.

"Who has heard such a thing? Who has seen such things? Shall the earth be made to give birth in one day? Or shall a nation be born at once? For as soon as Zion was in labor, She gave birth to her children." (Isaiah 66:8)

What an awesome God we serve! Since 1948, God has brought millions of Jewish people from the nations of the world back to the land of Israel.

"It shall come to pass in that day That the Lord shall set His hand again the second time To recover the remnant of His people who are left, From Assyria and Egypt, From Pathros and Cush, From Elam and Shinar, From Hamath and the islands of the sea."

(Isaiah 11:11)

As of December 2011, God has brought over seven million Jewish people back to the land of Israel. The world statistics note that there are around fourteen million Jewish people on the earth. For the first time in over 1900 years, almost fifty percent of the total world Jewish population is living inside the land

> When you pray for the peace of Jerusalem, you are praying for the Aliyah—the immigration of the Jewish people back to the land of Israel.

of Israel. What an incredible time we are living in to see the faithfulness of God unveiling in front of our eyes! This clearly indicates that Jesus is coming back to the earth very soon.

So when you pray for the peace of Jerusalem, you

are praying for the Aliyah—the immigration of the Jewish people back to the land of Israel. I strongly encourage you to pray and support this cause. It's the testimony of God's faithfulness to His promises and to His people.

> "Therefore behold, the days are coming, says the LORD, 'that it shall no more be said, The LORD lives who brought up the children of Israel from the land of Egypt,' but, 'The LORD lives who brought up the children of Israel from the land of the north and from all the lands where He had driven them.' For I will bring them back into their land which I gave to their fathers." (Jeremiah 16:14-15)

This is the heart of God. I would encourage you to plug into to it and reap its blessings.

## The Physical and Spiritual Zion Being Built

The Bible declares that God will build Zion; and then, He will come back. We read in Psalm 102:16, "For the LORD shall build up Zion; He shall appear in His glory." God is bringing back the scattered

> "The LORD builds up Jerusalem; He gathers together the outcasts of Israel." Psalm 147:2

Jewish people, building Jerusalem and Israel. At the same time He is also building the spiritual Zion, the Church. God is building by the power of the Holy Spirit both the physical and spiritual Zion.

As you pray for the peace of Jerusalem, you are actually accelerating the building of the physical and spiritual Zion and hasten His coming. I pray God will help you to understand the depth and the importance to pray for the peace of Jerusalem.

This is the quick caption of what we learned in this chapter. When we pray for the peace of Jerusalem, we are actually praying for the following:

1.  The second coming of Jesus Christ
2.  Salvation of the Jewish people
3.  Salvation of the nations
4.  Salvation of the Ishmaels (Arabs) and Muslims
5.  Aliyah – Jewish immigration to the land of Israel
6.  Building of the physical and spiritual Zion
7.  Hasten His coming

8. Above all, for a worldwide revival, this will lead to the rapture and culminate in the end of the age.

I encourage you to begin to pray for the peace of Jerusalem, enter into the pleasure and reward of God. God has promised peace and a blessed life, when we pray for the peace of Jerusalem. I strongly encourage you to make a commitment to pray daily and reap His blessings. As in Psalm 122:6-7, "Pray for the peace of Jerusalem: 'May they prosper who love you. Peace be within your walls, Prosperity within your palaces.'"

Make a practice to pray for the peace of Jerusalem every day while you pray before you eat. This way you don't forget. May the Lord bless you with His peace and blessed life, as you pray for the peace of Jerusalem!

## Chapter Five

# Blessing Israel: A Divine Way
# for a Blessed Life

As God's children, we need to get it deep down into our hearts that it is God's will for His children to be blessed with divine health and blessings. It is sad to see that many of us do not have this revelation. We just live as we are, not enjoying the life God intended for us. Jesus came to give us life and life in abundance.

All through the Bible, God has commanded us to obey Him in order to be blessed. One of these commandments is to pray for the peace of Jerusalem. He has promised to bless us abundantly, when we obey and pray.

We saw the importance of praying for the peace

of Jerusalem in the previous chapter. With this understanding, I have further attempted to explore the Scriptures to explain why we are blessed when we pray for the peace of Jerusalem.

**"Pray for the peace of Jerusalem: "May they prosper who love you. Peace be within your walls, Prosperity within your palaces." (Psalm 122:6-7) We will explore the meaning of three main words in this Scripture: peace, prosper, and prosperity.**

## 1. Peace:

**Peace is what you are praying for Jerusalem; and peace is what you receive.** In the above verse, peace is the Hebrew word is Shalom. The root word has the following meanings:

### a. Completeness

When you pray for the peace of Jerusalem, He has promised completeness in number. You will live the days allotted by the Almighty God to you. The promise, in Deuteronomy 33:25, will come to pass in your life. "Your sandals shall be iron and bronze; As your days, so shall your strength be."

## b. Soundness

He has promised the soundness of the body. Divine health is His standard for His children. God has promised to give you divine health, when you pray for the peace of Jerusalem.

## c. Welfare

He has promised welfare. The New Webster Dictionary defines welfare as the state of being healthy, happy and free from want. Wow! This is what the people are striving and working hard for. Your God has promised to give you this, when you pray for the peace of Jerusalem. Your God will support you day by day, in Psalm 68:19, "Blessed be the Lord, Who daily loads us with benefits, The God of our salvation! Selah."

## d. Peace

The peace here means not only peace in your heart and mind, but also in your human relationships and internal strives, etc. You will also be in a covenant relationship with God. Do you really need peace in your family, job, ministry, finances and every aspect of your life? Then pray daily for the peace of Jerusalem and receive this promise of God.

### e. Quiet, Tranquility, and Contentment

Shalom also means quiet, tranquility. In this world filled with chaos and confusion, God has promised quietness and tranquility amidst the world's turmoil. The word, tranquil means free from agitation, peaceful, or a state of calmness.

Contentment is a great struggle in the culture today. The Bible declares, in Timothy 6:6, "Now godliness with contentment is great gain." Contentment will protect you from much heartache. God has promised it, when you pray for the peace of Jerusalem.

### 2. Prosper:

The next word I want to focus on from this Scripture is to prosper. When you love Jerusalem, a blessing to prosper rests upon you. The Hebrew word for prosper is Shala. The meanings for Shala are:

### a. Be at Ease

Job portrays the condition of the modern world so beautifully. Everywhere you turn is trouble, in Job 3:26, "I am not at ease, nor am I quiet; I have no rest, for trouble comes."

This is the state of the unbelievers at large, including many Christians around the world. The world is heading towards its darkest, most troubled conditions in the history of the human race. We all need this state of ease, quiet and rest. This is available and kept in store for those who pray for the peace of Jerusalem.

### b. Successful

Everyone wants to be successful. People work hard and do whatever it takes to be successful. Most of the time, we are not able to achieve what we aim for. We become discouraged and frustrated. Some Christians even lose the joy of salvation and drift away from God. But God has promised success, when we pray for the peace of Jerusalem.

In Proverbs 10:22, we read, "The blessing of the LORD makes one rich, And He adds no sorrow with it." Only the blessings of the Lord will not add sorrow to it. His blessings will give us the ability to enjoy life, under the Biblical guidance and be successful.

## c. Secure, to be Safe

To prosper means secure or to be safe. If money is everything, why do some successful people, celebrities and very rich people get frustrated and end up committing suicide? Though we might have everything, it is God's grace that helps us to enjoy our life with secured minds and in safety. The word secure or to be safe actually means for one to securely enjoy prosperity. This is what God has promised, when we pray for the peace of Jerusalem.

Are you getting the picture, why people are blessed when they began to pray for the peace of Jerusalem? There is still the word prosperity to explore.

## 3. Prosperity:

I would like to iron out the attitude of the Christians toward this word prosperity. I would like to emphasize, when Psalm 122 says *prosperity*, it is not only about the material prosperity according to the world's standard. Prosperity has a much deeper meaning than we think. It is not just about money. I will attempt to give the meaning of prosperity according to the Scripture.

The real prosperity is divine health, nothing wanting, nothing broken, and fruitful in due seasons. Irrespective of your bank balance, your needs and desires are supplied supernaturally. You will be a channel of blessings and not a reservoir.

The greatest example of this is the life of the Israelites in the wilderness. The Bible declares that it literally took no effort, except their obedience to God to run their life without any lack.

- There was no one sick among the millions of Jews.
- Their clothes did not wear out.
- Their sandals did not tear.
- They had supernatural cooling and heating systems.

- They were given room service with heavenly manna and quail.
- Waters gushed out of rocks and deserts, when they needed.

With this in mind, I would like to illustrate what this word prosperity means. The word prosperity in this Scripture in Hebrew is the derivative from Shalah. It means:

## a. Abundance, Prosperity

Paul describes abundance so beautifully in 2 Corinthians 9:8, "And God is able to make all grace abound toward you, that you, always having all sufficiency in all things, may have an abundance for every good work."

God will generously provide all our needs, so that we will always be able to bless others. We will be ready for anything and everything that God wants us to do. God has promised prosperity for everyone who fears Him and serves Him. In fact, in 2 Corinthians 8:9, Jesus took our poverty and through His poverty, we become rich.

I hope you got the picture about prosperity from God's perspective. God wants you to have a blessed life. As you understand, in Job 36:11, "If they obey and serve Him, They shall spend their days in prosperity, And their years in pleasures."

## b. Quietness, Peaceable

Prosperity also means quietness or peaceable. The Bible teaches that the human heart tends to become proud and arrogant, due to abundance of wealth. All through the Scriptures, we see people forget God, when they became blessed, which led to their down fall. The great example is King Solomon. He was the richest man that ever lived on the earth; yet his end was so sad.

"When you have eaten and are full.... Beware that you do not forget the LORD your God...lest when you have eaten and are full, and have built beautiful houses and dwell in them...and when your herds and your flocks multiply...and your silver and your gold are multiplied...when your heart is lifted up, and you forget the LORD your God...then you say in your heart, 'My power and the might of my hand have gained me this wealth'" (Deuteronomy 8:10-17)

God warns us of our human heart's frailty. We must always remember that God is our provider and the only source.

You will be quiet and peaceful, trusting God, despite your success and wealth, when you pray for the peace of Jerusalem. What an awesome promise and safe place to live prosperously without offending God. You will live in contentment, when you trust in God.

### c. Wholeness

Many of us, when it comes to prosperity, only think of money. However, this is just one slice of it. Jesus explains this in Revelation 3:17, "Because you say, 'I am rich, have become wealthy, and have need of nothing' — and do not know that you are wretched, miserable, poor, blind, and naked".

One might have millions of dollars in his

bank account, but be dying of cancer. He is prosperous in finances, not in health. In the same way, one might have divine health, but not have a dime in his bank account. He is not prosperous either. Yet, another might have divine health and money, but poor in his habits because of bondages, addictions, etc.

"Beloved, I pray that you may prosper in all things and be in health, just as your soul prospers," **as affirmed in** 3 John 1:2. God wants us to prosper in our spirit, soul, and body. This is what wholeness means. God has promised to give us prosperity in all areas of our lives. This is what divine prosperity is all about.

I encourage you to pray for the peace of Jerusalem and enter into the fullness of the God's blessings.

# Chapter Six

# Why Are We Blessed When We Bless the Jewish People and Bless Israel?

It is very clear that God blesses and prospers us, when we pray for the peace of Jerusalem. Christians at large wanted to bless the Jewish people and the land of Israel, in order to get blessed according to the promise in Genesis 12:1-3. But many of us do not know the true reason why we are blessed. What does the Scripture say about this? Here, I have attempted to scripturally shed some light on this fact. First, we need to consider the covenant God made with Abraham.

"Now the LORD had said to Abram: "Get out of your country, From your family And from your father's house, To a land that I will show you. I will make you a great nation; I will bless you And make your name great; And you shall be a blessing. I will bless those who bless you, And I will curse him who curses you; And in you all the families of the earth shall be blessed." (Genesis 12:1-3)

God made a covenant with Abraham, whoever blesses him and his descendants will be blessed; whoever curses him will be cursed. God was so impressed with Abraham's obedience, when he did not withhold his only son Isaac. So, God blessed Abraham and made an everlasting covenant of blessing.

"By Myself I have sworn, says the LORD, because you have done this thing, and have not withheld your son, your only son...blessing I will bless you, and multiplying I will multiply your descendants as the stars of the heaven and as the sand which [is] on the seashore; and your descendants shall possess the gate of their enemies. In your seed all the nations of the earth shall be blessed, because you have obeyed My voice." (Genesis 22:16-18)

The key words in this verse are:
- Blessing and multiplying
- Possess the gate of the enemy
- His seed will be a blessing to all the nations of the earth

Here, we see God blessing Abraham and progressively moving towards the defeat of Satan on the cross by Jesus Christ, who came through the lineage of Abraham. Finally Jesus, Abraham's seed, will be a blessing to all the nations of the earth through His death, burial, and resurrection. There is no other name than the name of Jesus Christ, the son of Abraham, of the tribe of Judah through which the human race is redeemed. "Now to Abraham and his Seed were the promises made. He does not say, "And to seeds," as of many, but as of one, "And to your Seed," who is Christ," written in Galatians 3:15.

Abraham got the revelation of the gospel many years before he obeyed and offered Isaac. In fact, the Bible declares that the gospel was preached in advance to Abraham. In Galatians 3:8, we read, "And the Scripture, foreseeing that God would justify the Gentiles by faith, preached the gospel to Abraham beforehand, saying, "In you all the nations shall be blessed."

Many of us might wonder, "When was the gospel preached to Abraham?" In Genesis 14, when Abraham defeated his enemies, he was met by Melchizedek, King of Salem.

"Then Melchizedek king of Salem brought <u>out bread and wine</u>; he was the priest of God Most High. And he blessed him and said: '<u>Blessed be Abram of God Most High</u>, Possessor of heaven and earth; And blessed be God Most High, Who has delivered your enemies into your hand.' <u>And he gave him a tithe of all.</u>"
(Genesis 14:18-20)

Jesus Christ appeared as Melchizedek, preached the gospel to Abraham, and revealed to him the shedding of His blood for the remission of the sins of the world—Jesus' body would be broken for the welfare of the believers. Jesus Christ gave communion to

Abraham and sealed the covenant of blessing; and Abraham gave Him a tithe.

The appearance of Jesus, during the Old Testament times, is called 'Christophany.' Christophany is the appearance, or non-physical manifestation of Jesus Christ. Did you get the picture? The believers take the communion, give a tithe to Jesus as an act of surrender and expression of total dependence on God for their daily living.

How do we know that Melchizedek is Jesus Christ? Apostle Paul clarifies it and confirms it.

"For this Melchizedek, king of Salem, priest of the Most High God, who met Abraham returning from the slaughter of the kings and blessed him, to whom also Abraham gave a tenth part of all, first being translated 'king of righteousness,' and then also king of Salem, meaning 'king of peace,' without father, without mother, without genealogy, having neither beginning of days nor end of life, but made like the Son of God, remains a priest continually." (Hebrews 7:1-3)

Since Paul has explained this so beautifully, I don't think we need any more explanation. Now, it is clear that the gospel came through the Jews. Jesus Himself declared this with His own mouth, when He was preaching the gospel to a Gentile Samaritan woman, in John 4:21. "You worship what you do not know; we know what we worship, for salvation is of the Jews."

Do you understand? When you bless the Jewish people, you are actually blessing the gospel. This is one of the primary reasons you are blessed, when you bless the Jewish people. When you believe in Jesus, you are becoming the spiritual descendants of Abraham.

"So then those who are of faith are blessed with believing Abraham." (Galatians 3:9)

"For you are all sons of God through faith in Christ Jesus. For as many of you as were baptized into Christ have put on Christ. There is neither Jew nor Greek, there is neither slave nor free, there is neither male nor female; for you are all one in Christ Jesus. And if you are

Christ's, then you are Abraham's seed, and heirs according to the promise."

(Galatians 3:26-29)

We all are one in Christ Jesus. We are actually plugging into the anointing of God's blessed covenant with Abraham and the gospel. God made covenant with Abraham for blessing those who bless him and cursing those who curse him. This covenant is very powerful; and I want to explain little more.

God promises to be a friend to Abraham's friends, to take the kindnesses shown to Abraham as it was done to God Himself; and He will recompense them accordingly. God will take care that none will be losers, by any service done for his people.

We read, in Numbers 22-24, the story of Balaam and King Balak. Balaam was hired by king Balak to curse Jewish people. But Balaam realized that God has pleasure in blessing the Jewish people.

"...Balaam saw that it pleased the LORD to bless Israel." (Numbers 24:1)

"And God said to Balaam, 'You shall not go

119

with them; you shall not curse the people, for they are blessed.'" (Numbers 22:12)

God has said that the Jewish people are blessed, period. There are no more arguments. It is clear, when we bless the Jewish people, we will be blessed by God. We have great examples throughout the Bible of how God has blessed those who blessed the Jewish people.

## Old Testament Examples

### Abimelech

In Genesis 20, we read the story of Abraham and Abimelech. When Abimelech blessed Abraham with sheep, oxen, male, female servants, and also restored Sarah to Abraham. We see God's blessing come to Abimelech's household. "Then Abimelech took sheep, oxen, and male and female servants and gave them to Abraham; and he restored Sarah his wife to him," in Genesis 20:14.

Abimelech, his wife and all his female servants were barren. God healed them all, when

Abraham prayed and released the blessings. Later they bore children.

> "So Abraham prayed to God; and God healed Abimelech, his wife, and his female servants. Then they bore children; for the Lord had closed up all the wombs of the house of Abimelech because of Sarah, Abraham's wife." (Genesis 20:17-18)

Here we see the covenant of blessing operating powerfully. The curse of barrenness is reversed and blessings flowed.

## Rahab

Rahab was a prostitute in the city of Jericho. When Joshua sent the spies to spy out the land, she hid them and showed them favor, Joshua 2. She did an act of kindness to the Jewish people.

When God delivered Jericho into the hands of the Jewish people, He remembered Rahab and her household. They were the only survivors in the whole city of Jericho. Every person perished except her family. We read, in Joshua 6:25, "And Joshua spared Rahab the harlot, her father's household, and all that she had. So she dwells in Israel to this day, because she hid the messengers whom Joshua sent to spy out Jericho."

God remembered the covenant He made with Abraham. He completely reversed the curse of being a prostitute to a blessed mother. This Gentile woman became an ancestor of the Messiah Jesus Christ himself, as written in Matthew 1:5.

## Ammonite and Moabite:

In Deuteronomy 23, we read God's command to exclude the Ammonites and Moabites from the assembly of the Israelites. When the Israelites journeyed from Egypt to the Promised Land, the Ammonites and Moabites refused to meet the needs of the Jewish people.

We read, in Deuteronomy 23:4, "because they did not meet you with bread and water on the road when you came out of

Egypt, and because they hired against you Balam, the son of Beor from Pethor of Mesopotamia, to curse you."

They did not bless the Jewish people, rather, they planned to curse them; and instead, a curse came upon them.

"An Ammonite or Maobite shall not enter the assembly of the Lord; even to the tenth generation none of his descendants shall enter the assembly of the Lord forever."

(Deuteronomy 23:3)

"You shall not seek their peace nor their prosperity all your days forever."

(Deuteronomy 23:6)

Do you understand the magnitude of this covenant of blessing and cursing with the Jewish people? Praise God for our Lord Jesus Christ who took all the curses and shed His blood to destroy the middle wall of separation. Through His blood, you are a spiritual descendant of Abraham and all are equal in

Christ Jesus.

## New Testament Examples

### Roman Centurion

We read in Luke 7, when Jesus went to Capernaum, a Roman centurion's servant was ill. The centurion heard that Jesus was coming; and he sent Jewish leaders to plead with Jesus to come and heal his servant. The words the Jewish leaders used were very intriguing, which made Jesus immediately respond to them.

> "So when he heard about Jesus, he sent elders of the Jews to Him, pleading with Him to come and heal his servant. And when they came to Jesus, <u>they begged Him earnestly, saying that the one for whom He should do this was deserving, 'for he loves our nation, and has built us a synagogue. Then Jesus went with them</u>....'"
>
> (Luke 7: 3- 6)

Jesus acknowledged his work, acted swiftly to answer the centurion's request. Jesus was quick to bless a person who blessed the Jewish people. God is a covenant keeping God; His words are ever settled in the heavens.

### Cornelius

It is really amazing to realize that Pentecost came to the Gentiles, through a Gentile who loved and blessed the Jewish people. On the day of Pentecost, the outpouring of the Holy Spirit first came upon only the Jewish disciples of Jesus Christ. But, God chose the house of Cornelius to bring Pentecost to the Gentiles. The Scripture shows us the reason why God selected him.

> "And they said, "Cornelius the centurion, a just man, one who fears God and has a good reputation among all the nation of the Jews.... 'Cornelius, your prayer has been heard, and your alms are remembered in the sight of God.'" (Acts 10:22, 31)

Cornelius had a good reputation among the Jews. He was blessing the Jewish people, through his humanitarian help to the needy Jews.

## Brief History of the Nations Blessed or Cursed:

I want to bring to your attention a few nations, which are blessed because of blessing the Jewish people. Also, some nations who fell from their fame into a curse, because of their unsupportive anti-Semitic attitude towards the Jewish people.

## Egypt

Let's begin with ancient Egypt. It was at its peak when Joseph, the Jew, was the Prime Minister. Pharaoh honored Joseph's whole family. Egypt was prospering well. It was the greatest nation on the planet, during that time in history. But when Joseph died, the new Pharaoh, who did not know Joseph, began to oppress the Jewish people. Pharaoh and his army were destroyed; they drowned, while the Jewish people were delivered. Since then, the nation of Egypt has completely declined;

even now, it is in great chaos.

## Spain

The Spanish Empire was very huge. There were many Jewish people living and leading a good life there. At the peak of its power, it was one of the largest empires in the world's history, spanning Europe, the Americas, Africa, and Asia. It lasted from the fifteenth century through the latter portion of the twentieth century.

In 1481, the Inquisition of the Jews started in Spain. They systematically expelled the Jewish people from Spain. Since then, the decline began; and now we know the state of Spain. Missionaries say that Spain is one of the most difficult countries for evangelism in Europe.

I firmly believe, when the pastors and leaders in Spain gather together, seek forgiveness, and repent on behalf of their country for cursing the Jewish people, God will forgive, break open, the evangelism will increase, and multitudes will come into the Kingdom.

## Great Britain

At its peak, the British Empire was the largest formal empire that the world had ever known. Its power and influence stretched all over the globe. It influenced the world in many ways. Many Jewish people, who lived all over Great Britain, had peaceful lives and were prospering.

Israel, the West Bank, Gaza Strip, and Jordan were among many former Ottoman Arab territories placed under the administration of Great Britain by the League of Nations. The mandate lasted from 1920 to 1948. In 1917, Arthur Balfour decreed that the British would help Israel and the Jewish people to return to their land. But in 1939 the British broke the promise; instead, of helping the Jewish people, they agreed to partition the land into two states, Arab and Jewish. I believe the downfall of the British Empire began, when they chose not to bless Israel by breaking their promise to them.

The outworking of the curse can be clearly seen in the current state of the United Kingdom.

It is now becoming highly dominated by the Muslim population. Many large Churches and Cathedrals are being sold. Many banks and gas stations are bought by the radical Muslims and funding terrorists.

## United States of America

Columbus set sail on August 3, 1492, a day after the expulsion of the Jews from Spain began. Many believe that Columbus was Jewish and many of those who accompanied his first voyage were too. It has been said that the funding for the whole voyage was done by the Jewish businessmen. Even the technical expertise for the voyage was given by the Jewish people. The primary reason for this voyage was to find a safe haven for the Jewish people; since they were persecuted elsewhere.

Since the founding of this great nation, millions of Jewish have lived and prospered here. Above all, USA was the greatest ally and supporter from the first day Israel was re-established as a nation. Do you understand why the USA is the most prosperous country in the whole world so far? It is all because she is continuously blessing Israel. We all need to pray that the USA will maintain this position of blessing Israel and continue to be a world leader.

## India

India was under the rule of the British Empire. Even after her independence, India was struggling economically and about to declare bankrupt. It was due to the continuous unfriendly attitude towards Israel, of the different administrations since its independence. But today, India is an emerging economic power; and God is blessing India both spiritually and economically.

It all began in 1992, when India began to support by establishing full Diplomatic Relations with Israel. The trade partnership with Israel dates back to the time of Solomon. Today India and Israel enjoy an extensive economic, military, and diplomatic relationship. India is the second largest military partner of Israel after the Russian Federation. No wonder India is blessed now. India has grown to be one of the world leaders in the Software industry. Blessing Israel has brought a great blessing to the nation of India.

We can give numerous examples; and history has repeated itself. Many nations were blessed because they blessed Israel and were cursed because they cursed Israel. I hope I made it clear—we are blessed, when we bless the Jewish people and the land of Israel.

## Christians Are Indebted to Bless Israel

Whether we want to be blessed or not, Apostle Paul declares that it is our duty to bless the Jewish people.

"For it pleased those from Macedonia and Achaia to make a certain contribution for the poor among the saints who are in Jerusalem. It pleased them indeed, and they are their debtors. For if the Gentiles have been partakers of their spiritual things, their duty is also to minister to them in material things."

(Romans 15:26-27)

We are in debt to the Jewish people, as we have been partakers of their spiritual inheritance.

"...who are Israelites, to whom pertain the adoption, the glory, the covenants, the giving of the law, the service of God, and the promises; of whom are the fathers and from whom, according to the flesh, Christ came, who is over all, the eternally blessed God. Amen."

(Romans 9:4-5)

As we partook in their spiritual things, Paul writes that we are in debt to them. It is the legitimate duty of every Christian to bless the Jewish people materially, in addition to praying for their salvation.

I encourage you to stand resolute in prayer and support of Israel. Israel needs a lot of support from her friends and allies. Her greatest ally at these end times is the believers in the body of Christ around the world.

Begin to bless Israel and enter into the pleasure of the Lord. You will reap the blessings of Abraham physically and the spiritual outpouring on your life. In Galatians 3:14, it reads, "that the blessing of Abraham might come upon the Gentiles in Christ Jesus, that we might receive the promise of the Spirit through faith." **God bless you!**

# Chapter Seven

# An Invitation to Get Involved in Preparing the Way for the King of Glory

God raised John the Baptist to prepare the way for Jesus Christ, when He came the first time. Now God is raising you and me, with the spirit of Elijah, to prepare the way for the King of Glory to come for the second time.

There are several ways you can get involved in preparing the way. The greatest way, apart from preaching the gospel, is to pray for the peace of Jerusalem, financially bless the Jewish people and the land of Israel.

You can get involved in the following ways. Whichever way God is calling you or you choose to be involved, be assured that you will be blessed mightily and hasten His coming as well.

1. Pray for the peace of Jerusalem on a daily basis.
2. Invite us to conduct a conference in your church or for a group in your city/nation.
3. Open your home for a Bible study to teach about praying for the peace of Jerusalem, and raise up an army to intercede for Israel.
4. Be an ambassador for Israel in your church and community. With your Pastor's permission, begin 'A Day of Prayer for Jerusalem' in your congregation.
5. Take a tour of Israel.
6. Physically volunteer with a Christian or Jewish organization in Israel. They need our help.
7. Financially support Christian ministries and organizations in Israel. Since the body of Christ in Israel is very small, they have a great need and look for support from the nations.
8. Pray and support Aliyah—the Jewish

immigration to the land of Israel. Many Jewish people need finances to go through this process.

9. Pray and financially support the Jewish and Arab pastors and leaders.

10. Pray and support organizations involved in humanitarian aid to Israel. They need a lot of help due to frequent terrorist attacks.

11. Reach out to the Jews in your community with the love of Christ. They long for someone to love them, as they have faced many persecutions for many centuries from Christians and others alike.

We, the Gentiles, are called to provoke the Jewish people to jealousy and turn to their Messiah. The nations are called to be the fathers and mothers to care and nurture the Jewish people spiritually.

"Thus says the Lord God: 'Behold, I will lift My hand in an oath to the nations, And set up My standard for the peoples; They shall bring your sons in their arms, And your daughters shall be carried on their shoulders; Kings shall be your fathers, And their queens your nursing mothers...." (Isaiah 49:22-23)

The nations are called to help the Jewish people go back to their land and to their Messiah. God is calling each one of us to work closely in any of the ways listed above to prepare the way for the King of Glory.

God has called our ministry to proclaim that the King is coming to the nations. The conference I conduct is entitled: "The King is Coming: Pray for the Peace of Jerusalem." The teachings provided through the conference and this book has been a great blessing for many pastors, leaders, and believers.

We encourage you to contact us. We will help you reach out to the particular ministry you are called to support. We work closely to bless the nation of Israel; and we have extensive connections in Israel.

May the God of Israel bless you abundantly, according to His promise, as you stand in support of Israel. The King is coming; pray for the peace of Jerusalem!

# Bibliography

1. Derek Prince, *Our Debt to Israel.* (Derek Prince Ministries International, 1984).

2. Tom Hess, *Pray for the Peace of Jerusalem.* (Progressive Vision International, 2001).

3. John Hagee, *In Defense of Israel.* (FrontLine, A Strang Company, 2007).

4. Keith Intrater & Dan Juster, Israel, *The Church and The Last Days* (Destiny Image Publishers Inc., 2003).

5. James W. Goll, *Praying for Israel's Destiny* Chosen, A Division of Baker Publishing Group,

2005. http://elijahlist.com/words/display_word.html?ID=9641. Web

6. Chuck Missler. "Mysteries Behind Our History: Was Columbus Jewish?" http://www.khouse.org/articles/1996/109/

7. Rob Eshman. "Was Christopher Columbus a Jew?" http://www.jewishjournal.com/bloggish/item/was_christopher_columbus_a_jew_20091012/.

We Bless Israel, "Historical Evidence that God Keeps His promises Regarding Those Who Bless and Curse Israel" http://weblessisrael.org/historical_evidence.html

# About the Author

S am Dewald Stephen is an ordained minister and
founding Pastor of World Healing International
Church, an evangelistic; Spirit empowered Church
in Arlington, Texas.

He was born in India, accepted the call of God
and entered into the ministry as Administrator of
Derek Prince Ministries, India.

In 2005, God called him and his family to Israel.
He served as the Administrator for Jerusalem House
of Prayer for All Nations in Jerusalem, Israel, a
24-hour house of prayer dedicated to pray for Israel
and all Nations.

In 2008, Sam and his family moved to Texas from
Israel in obedience to the call of God to be missionaries to the United States.

It was while living in Israel, God imparted to Pastor Sam the specifics concerning "Why we should pray for the peace of Jerusalem". Since then, it has become Sam's passion to educate churches and leaders about this truth. He conducts 'The King is coming – Pray for the Peace of Jerusalem' Conference all across America.

He is also an adjunct Lecturer in Christ For the Nations Bible Institute, Dallas, Texas.

He has traveled to many countries to proclaim the healing and saving power of our Lord Jesus Christ.

Sam is a graduate of the Advanced Leadership and Pastoral School at Christ for the Nations Institute (CFNI) in Dallas, Texas. He also holds a Master's Degree in Business Administration, Bachelor's in Computer Science and an Advanced Diploma as 'International Travel Consultant from IATA/UFTAA, Geneva, Switzerland.

Sam and his wife, Suganthi, have been married for 16 years and are blessed with a son and a daughter.

# Order and Contact Information

Get your copy at Amazon, Barnes & Noble or contact us.

Contact Information:
Pastor Sam Dewald Stephen
www.whichurch.org
pastordewald@gmail.com
817-845-3616

CPSIA information can be obtained
at www.ICGtesting.com
Printed in the USA
FFOW04n1553120314
4213FF

9 781622 306145